Advancing the Kingdom through Entrepreneurship & Marketplace Leadership

Write It Out
PUBLISHING, LLC

VIRGINIA BEACH, VA

Copyright © September 2023 Kiyanni Bryan

All rights reserved. This document is geared towards providing exact and reliable information with regard to the topic and issue covered. The publication is sold with the idea that the publisher is not required to render accounting, officially permitted, or otherwise, qualified services. If advice is necessary, legal or professional, a practiced individual in the profession should be ordered.

No part of this publication may be reproduced, duplicated, distributed, or transmitted in any form or by any means, including photocopying, recording, or other electronic or mechanical methods, without the prior written permission of the publisher, except in the case of brief quotations embodied in critical reviews and certain other non-commercial uses permitted by copyright law. Recording of this publication is strictly prohibited and any storage of this document is not allowed unless with written permission from the publisher. All rights reserved.

The information provided herein is stated to be truthful and consistent, in that any liability, in terms of inattention or otherwise, by any usage or abuse of any policies, processes, or directions contained within is the solitary and utter responsibility of the recipient reader. Under no circumstances will any legal responsibility or blame be held against the publisher for any reparation, damages, or monetary loss due to the information herein, either directly or indirectly.

Respective authors own all copyrights not held by the publisher.

Printed by Kiyanni B., Write It Out Publishing LLC. in the United States of America.

Write It Out Publishing LLC
Virginia Beach, Virginia
Writeitoutpublishing.com

ISBN: 979-8-9874539-9-5

Book Cover Illustrator: Maurice Rogers
Editor: Renee Johnson and Tamira K. Butler-Likely
First printing, (e-book or paperback) September 30th, 2023

Visionary Kiyanni Bryan
Virginia Beach, VA 23452
Writeitoutpub@gmail.com
Kiyannibryan.com

KINGDOM BUILDERS

Advancing the Kingdom through Entrepreneurship & Marketplace Leadership

ARCHITECTS

Kiyanni Bryan | Gary Ellick | Dr. Charlene D Winley
Robert Bennett | Elouise Townsend | Andre Mason
Ciara Mason | Erica Ojada | Dr. Chavon Anette
Justin Goodman | Luis Trochez | Lakia Perez

Foreword Torace Solomon | Prologue Jeff Wittaker

Table of contents

Dedication..9

Acknowledgements....................................11

Foreword..13

Prologue..15

Intro..19

Visionary Kiyanni Bryan

Chapter 1	Conviction for the Assignment...................25
Chapter 2	Character for the Call...............................31
Chapter 3	Lead in Grace...39
	Leadership 101.......................................41

Architects

Elouise Townsend	Authentic Leadership.................................45
Luis Trochez	The Blueprint..49
Lakia Perez	Graced for It...55
Justin Goodman	Two Left Feet...59
Ciara Mason	Jumping the Hurdles of Opposition...........65
Dr. Chavon Anette	Trust the Architect....................................69
Gary Ellick	Build the Team, Achieve the Dream..........73
Dr. Charlene Winley	Be UNIQUELY You!..................................77
Robert Bennet Jr.	F.A.T - Faithful-Available-Teachable...........81
Erica Ojada	A Builder's Time & Grace..........................85
Andre Mason	NEXT...89

Dedication

To my mother, Elouise Townsend, who was my first life and business coach, thank you for your wisdom, love, knowledge, and support over the years. I have learned so much from you of "how" to lead effectively and in love. I pray this compilation makes you proud.

To my daughter, Ryanna Savonne Rickelle Rolling, I pray grace, strength, and boldness to you as you become the leader that God has called you to be.

To the reader, fellow "Leader," I want you to know that since you are here a shift is taking place internally in you. Whether you are already leading or an emerging leader, there will be an impartation from the Father by the conclusion of this book. I pray that your days leading, whether in the marketplace or in the ministry, are filled with joy, as you understand the privilege and the honor that it is to lead. That is to lead. Remember that you've been called to make a difference, remember that you are, in fact, deserving of good things, and remember that being your authentic self is what will really make the difference. The only way the anointing will flow is if you be you, you don't have to split your personality to lead the people. Trust the process!

Love, Kiy

Acknowledgements

Projects of this magnitude take time and support to accomplish. I want to take the time out to say thank you to every architect that contributed to this project, thank you to my staff at Write It Out Publishing LLC and thank you to every leader that ALLOWED me to Lead. Your prayers and continual support is appreciated and honored.

I thank God for each of you.

Kiyanni B.

Foreword

Building, on any level, is a wildly misjudged job. The hours, the money, the late nights, the long days, the obstacles, the preparation, the losses, and the fluctuating stress assigned to one called to build can never be put into words. We are in a society that demands so much from us. There is constant pressure to create and construct. The pressure is not only damaging, but divine. The demand on builders is both painful and purposeful. This is why many don't complete the tasks.

God has put something inside each of us. The world needs it, so He pressures us to build it. Builders in every sphere of influence are fueled by the unseen, fixed on the need, and inspired by the possibilities created by what they produce.

I believe this book will be an excellent resource and encouragement to anyone building. May you be provoked, realigned, and grounded by the thought processes in the coming pages, and may you learn to wear the pressure to build like a badge of honor.

Torace Solomon[1]
www.toracesolomon.com

Prologue

When we consider the arena of entrepreneurship and marketplace leadership, some of the first things we think of are principles, performance, and productivity. We teach principles necessary for the success of our businesses and organizations, we empower others to perform at levels exceeding the norm, and we expect productive results from the investment of our time, talent, and treasures into our visions and dreams. Some would say, with these three components working effectively, success is inevitable. I would agree! Principles, performance, and productivity are key contributors to the success of leaders, businesses, and organizations.

However, permit me to add one additional component to the equation for success in entrepreneurship and marketplace leadership: passion and care for people. Humans are the Creator's greatest creation, His most valued asset. We mean the world to Him! As a consequence of our importance to Him, there is an expectation in the earth for us to steward our interconnectedness well. This means we must exercise intentionality in giving the best of ourselves to each other. From an entrepreneurial and marketplace leadership perspective, we must passionately seek to pour the purest form of our nature into the people we serve within our businesses and organizations.

People themselves need to know, who they are to a vision or dream outweighs what they do to make the vision or dream come to pass. When people feel passionately cared for and loved, it motivates them to give the best of who they are to what they are responsible for in a business or an organization. "But I pay them well!" you say! Yes, you do! However, generosity must go beyond a paycheck, a bonus, or a few gift cards. If we expect people to use their intellect and skillset to build what's in our heart, we must generously give of our love, our care, and our time to show them how much they mean to us. What does this look like?

Passionately loving and caring for those who serve our visions and dreams is simple. Create opportunities for conversation outside of the context of the business and/or organization. It shows concern for what's going on in the lives of the employees. "How are the kids?" "How are your personal goals and accomplishments coming along?" "How is your day going?" These are simple inquiries with huge impact. It reveals an interest in who people are rather than what they do.

When I founded Transformation Church VA in 2017, I placed a heavy emphasis on passionately loving those who served with me. I spent time with them, checked up on them, and worked hard to create a space where they were seen. As the organization grew, my focus transitioned from building relational equity to building systems for success. Don't get me wrong, systems are necessary for the longevity of any business or organization. However, systems don't sustain relationships,, passion and care for others do. More recently, as I was reflecting on the journey of our organization, I realized how principles, performance, and productivity had overshadowed interpersonal passion for people. Specifically, my investment into their personal lives.

Yes, I deeply love everyone who has committed to building with me. However, it's one thing to say you love people and another thing to make time to show them you do. As we prepare to enter a new season of our organization, I have committed to investing into the personal lives of those who work alongside me first, and then into their talents. Organizations are only as healthy as the relationships holding them together. If you want to get the best out of what you're building, focus on building the people within them first. It's the only way that what you are building will last.

As you began your journey through the wisdom expressed in this Anthology, let me leave you with the words of the Apostle Paul, spoken to a very gifted and thriving group of believers in Corinth. He says, as recorded in 1 Corinthians 13:1–7, using the Message Bible translation, "If I speak with human eloquence and angelic ecstasy but don't love, I'm nothing but the creaking of a rusty gate. If I speak

God's Word with power, revealing all his mysteries and making everything plain as day, and if I have faith that says to a mountain, 'Jump,' and it jumps, but I don't love, I'm nothing. If I give everything I own to the poor and even go to the stake to be burned as a martyr, but I don't love, I've gotten nowhere. So, no matter what I say, what I believe, and what I do, I'm bankrupt without love."

Family, principles, performance, and productivity matter! They really do! However, they work best when they are built on the platform of passion and care. Whatever you're building, build it on love! Everything else will follow!

Pastor Jeff Wittaker[2]

Intro

It used to be when I heard the word "leadership" there wasn't anything I could identify with. It seemed to be something that was so high and far away from me, to the point where I never even considered that it was something tangible to reach.

I never gave leadership much thought because most of my life, I've spent in transitional phases, moving from what I felt like was death to life, then, from surviving to existing, and then, from existing to actually living a life out loud that I could be proud of.

Through much hardship and challenging times over the years, I learned how to be very submissive because I was humbled by my circumstances. In areas where before there had been pride and self-preservation that really was defensive mechanisms, they were burned away by soul-crushing life situations.

I'm grateful for the journey that God has allowed me to endure, because truth be told, that humility is one of the greatest qualities and characteristics of a leader. I believe that it is humility that safeguards your heart from deception, and it keeps you in the place of depending and leaning on Jesus for direction and guidance.

I remember I had a season of life where I was being developed in intercession. It was a period of time after I made a decision to wholeheartedly follow the Lord and after my friend groups were sifted through my life consecration. For years I stayed on my knees in prayer. I always had a prayer life but in this particular season, I began to learn the power of my words, and I began to exercise my authority in praying for others. During that time I would pray for others more than I would pray for myself, and throughout that process it really allowed me to feel the burden of those I warred for. I learned how to seek His heart about those He told me to pray for, to the point of feeling the burden of His will for their lives.

All those years I spent crying out names and issues and making decrees, I now know that it was intercession. That phase of my life groomed and developed me to be the leader I became. If I had a guide to tell me how to become a great leader, never would I have thought that one of the key components to becoming a great leader is being a Prophetic Intercessor.

It was in intercession that I developed stamina and the capacity to be able to really love people. It was spending hours in prayer that I grew compassion for the brokenness of others. In the natural, I was an advocate and an ambassador for things I believed in. I carried that same disposition in prayer while I warred for others and became a warrior in the secret place.

Years of intercession led me to lead, and leading led me to build. Kingdom building will be the process by which you create and construct an infrastructure for kingdom advancement and kingdom use. Whenever we regard "building" in this book, it will be relative to the Kingdom of God.

I have been in a building season for the past few years, and I believe that's when the vision transitions to the next level of serving. You then serve at a greater capacity and on a higher scale. For years I have been the architect creating blueprints for myself and others, assisting them with their vision and being a midwife to purpose. Now, it goes to the next step of construction for a full build-out of kingdom projects and the building up, a.k.a. leading, of other kingdom builders.

A builder is one that...

Gathers, constructs, repairs, creates, develops, orchestrates, and oversees God's craftsmanship. They are seers, leaders, inventors, and architects that curate an infrastructure for the safe dwelling of others.

Why Is Building so Important?

> *Matthew 11:12*
> *From the days of John the Baptist until now the kingdom of heaven has suffered violence, and the violent take it by force.*

The truth is, there is a war between good and evil. It is Team Jesus and Team Darkness, and at some point, everyone will have to choose a side. If they decide not to choose, their default will be the latter.

In this day and time Satan has pulled out all stops possible to draft souls into hell, into darkness, forever separated from Christ. We as the body of Christ have a post and a responsibility to evangelize and spread the gospel of Jesus Christ in power and with authority. He saved our lives, and now our mandate becomes to go get others. Remember when it was your soul on the line, the Father wishes that no man perish (2 Peter 3:9).

We build by creating ministries and kingdom businesses, attacking every mountain of influence, planting churches, creating HUBS for spiritual development, writing books, and creating amazing leaders.

The expertise of skills of both the architect and builder is needed for the fulfillment, finding your place, and identifying your assignment. In this book, we will identify with "Builders," which encompasses the architect in us. We have work to do and IT'S TIME TO BUILD!

An architect purely deals with providing blueprints of the house design and how the finished product will look. A builder, on the other hand, uses the provided layout for reference during construction to ensure that no detail is missed.

Architects deal in abstract aspects and the overall design vision for your home. Builders work with the details, nuts, and bolts of construction. On new homes, especially custom or semi-custom homes, there is a need for both architectural and builder expertise

KIYANNI BRYAN[14]

Kiyanni B. is an Author, Life Strategist, Transformational Speaker, Publisher, Spiritual Midwife, Prophet, and Next Level Leadership Coach that specializes in helping leaders that have been impacted in the area of their identity THRIVE in kingdom life and business. As the owner of the following organizations: Kiyanni Impacts LLC, Write It Out Publishing LLC, and Shalema's Heart Association, she creates solutions and strategies that enable individuals to overcome their greatest obstacles with clarity, implementation, and accountability.

Chapter 1

Conviction for the Assignment

It starts here ... the grip and grasp of the heart.

After journeying with the Lord over periods of time, a few things take place while you grow in that relationship. You can experience the joy of salvation, the struggle to access newness, the suffering of the sacrifice to come up higher, and the inevitable discomfort of all the many transitions that you will endure over time.

Walking with the Lord is a journey that consists of constant transitions, but it is the greatest walk you will ever take in your lifetime. We often don't realize at the times that things occur that we are in a state of being made ready, some of our greatest obstacles of preparation for our next season.

As you mature in Christ you understand that at some point you will have to endure hardship, but even more so it will be "HIM" that could lead you into that place. Everything good and perfect comes from the Lord, but He is also fair and just (James 1:17). His ways are also higher than our ways and thoughts higher than our thoughts, so we won't always know "how" He wants to go about doing things, but as you grow you will trust Him to get it done.

> *Isaiah 55:8-9*
> *For my thoughts are not your thoughts, neither are your ways my ways, declares the LORD. For as the heavens are higher than the earth, so are my ways higher than your ways and my thoughts than your thoughts (ESV).*

Trust grows in every healthy relationship. It isn't a blanket action to trust the Lord, you may trust Him in some areas but others, not so much. Relationships take time and as you learn His character and receive His loving heart for you, the journey of trust itself will begin to grow.

You must be fully persuaded the Lord loves you in order to fulfill your life assignment. If there is doubt or lack of assuredly in your heart it will only slow you down as you build, and it will cause you to delay your obedience to His instructions.

The Assignment...

Do you know what your kingdom assignment is? For a long time I didn't know what mines was, so when I ask it's with the most sincerity of heart. I want you to know so you can be confident in how you build and maneuver.

People attempt to build without the clarity of the end goal because they don't know what the actual assignment is. By assignment, I mean your kingdom assignment, the thing that God has specifically designated and tasked you to do for the advancement of His kingdom. It means that it becomes your personal right and duty to fulfill because it has been assigned to your life as a post you should "man."

If you know your kingdom assignment, that's amazing, but if you don't, here is some wisdom to identify it and get started. I want you to take some time to do a self-evaluation by pondering and writing or journaling out the outcomes of your findings after you examine some of your circumstances. I want you to reflect on the following:

- What are your innate gifts and abilities? These things you do without regard are an endowment of being able to do something that comes naturally, you were born with the ability.

- What talents and skillsets do you possess? These are things you are amazing at with little training and cultivation, but you have a great foundational sense of them.

- What are your passions? These are your strong desires of what you like and believe in.

- What are your burdens? These are things that bring a sense of weight to your heart to the point that you are uncomfortable and can't seem to rest.

- What's in your hand? What are you currently doing? Where do you work? What are your streams of income? What do you do or have a desire to do in ministry?

If there was ONE THING that you would fix, correct, and/or adjust to make the body of Christ better ... what would that be?

Write these things out, pray it through, and ask God for direction on where to get started. Your assignment doesn't have to look like anyone else's because remember, your journey isn't like anyone else's. Once you identify something begin to move on it, doesn't matter how small you make think it is. It can be just ONE step, but do it because you will get more as you GO!

Never discredit that part of the process because you will need every part of it, nothing is wasted with the Lord. Your first step could be a wise Facebook post, a reel sharing your heart on a matter, or a blog post with information. Everything counts and helps to begin the building process.

My publishing company began from a small greeting card company idea where all I wanted to do was share little bits of encouragement to people in cards. I wanted to be the next Mahogany and be a faith-based company sharing Jesus as a way to touch people's hearts. It went from greeting cards to blogs, from blogs to my first book, from books to speaking engagements to my publishing company.

You never quite know where the first step will lead you, but it is critical that you take that step and get started. Once you get something to start with, create a layout and pray through strategy. Do it with all your heart and do it as unto the Lord.

> *Colossians 3:23*
> *And whatever you do, do it heartily, as to the Lord and not to men, knowing that from the Lord you will receive the reward of the inheritance; for you serve the Lord Christ (ESV).*

It will be imperative that you commit to making plans along the way, so you will have to spend some time dreaming through what the end goal looks like. If you don't see an end result to the build-out, how do you keep on task? How do you measure progress? And how do you stay accountable? A blueprint of what you are building will determine your success rate for completion.

We want to responsibly steward what the Lord gives us, so we manage every part of the process.

Preparation...

As a builder, you have gone through seasons of preparation to get to the place of laying a foundation for a build-out. Often times we as builders don't realize that God used EVERYTHING that we endured to prepare us for such a time as this.

I remember when I received the revelation that nothing is wasted with God, and it encouraged me in such a way that I was able to endure with greater faith. No matter the circumstances, the issue, the resistance, and what I could see with my natural eyes ... it became a sure thing that I loved Him, and I believed I was called according to His purposes.

> *Romans 8:28*
> *And we know that for those who love God, all things work together for good,[a] for those who are called according to his purpose (ESV).*

A lot of the things I was scared about when I began my building process were really obsolete, but I couldn't see it at that time. I was already doing the majority of those things anyway, the only difference was now I was going to be "intentional" and "accountable" for it by creating a plan around it. Giving it structure placed pressure on me and I began to get nervous, questioning my ability to do something that I was already doing.

It's amazing how the mind works, but I need you to know it's fear-based reservations that hold you back, so receive the truth so you can get started.

Conviction ...

We walked through the assignment and the readiness to get here to the conviction of it all. A heartfelt conviction will be the thing that propels you, pulls you, and pushes you into action like you would never believe. It consists of an internal resolve of an opinion and attitude about how you see something, a belief that is so internally compelling it spills out and over into your life and actions.

When I first began to feel a conviction for certain things, I didn't know what it was. I was so uncomfortable and literally almost tormented by the thought of what bothered me, to a degree of loss of sleep and constant meditation on it. I began to feel the weight of my assignment in such a way that I had no choice but to do something about it because it became literal agony to stand by and watch.

Knowing something in our minds isn't enough. We can know something and not do anything about it, we can believe something and not put it into action, which is what faith is all about. My desire over the years had been not to just believe in God but to give Him my life by faith, to not just know something in my mind but to heed to the point of submission and obedience to His voice.

We as builders should carry a burden for the assignment. It should never be addressed or approached nonchalantly and without deep concern. We take ownership of it and make it our responsibility as the Lord assigns it to us. Ultimately, we submit to the high calling of Jesus Christ and walk out the path of whatever that looks like for our individual lives.

> *"My prayer is that your head knowledge becomes a heart conviction."*

Chapter 2

Character for the Call

"Character is the foundation of the builder and determines the weight and depth of the build-out."

Going to church every Sunday of my life was completely normal. I attended a small Baptist church in Harlem that was owned and managed by my family. My Sundays consisted of early morning Sunday school, preparation in the church for Sunday service, watching my granduncle/grandfather prepare for his sermon, and finding my friends to sit with in service. That was, of course, if I didn't have to usher with my grandmother.

I sometimes had to sing a solo and definitely jumped to any opportunity to sing with the children's choir. We stayed in the church for long periods of time and sometimes went to other churches for after services to join in worship with them. Yep, church was a major part of my life and I didn't know anything different. Although the church was a norm and I knew how to carry myself, how to respond, and how to act outside of church, those norm behaviors did not exist.

I gave my life to the Lord at eight years old, the "first" time. I was sitting in one of those services and my grandfather gave the altar call. I heard the Lord call me so I got up and went. He patted me on the head and smiled, and as he continued with the altar call moment every other child in that church followed me and came to stand behind me in that moment. We all got baptized together. I didn't realize it then, but God was showing me the leader in me.

At that age, I didn't know how to live and tried my best to be a good girl. I remember feeling bad when doing things I shouldn't do and KNOWING that I was wrong. I would feel so guilty and tell the Lord I'm sorry. Over the years, from that age through my teen years, I would learn some hard truths in life. Even in my twenties I was constantly back sliding due to a lack of faith and understanding of who I was and really "whom" I belonged to.

I believe a major part of a person having good character is them knowing who they are and being assured in identity. I didn't know who I was outside of pain, and my name become "victim." Sometimes we can get addicted to our story and lose sight of the purpose of why God allowed the circumstance.

Part of the journey to your life's purpose has to do with your identity, and your identity can only be solidified in Christ. As you draw to Him and get to know Him, He shows you, YOU. Isn't He just a loving Father, everything always comes back around to ensure we have what we need. (Smiles)

It's Real...

Growing up, I lived in the house with my grandmother, mother, aunts, and cousins. Right next door there were more aunts, uncles, and cousins, which was great. My family is fairly large on both sides and I'm grateful I'm close to the majority, meaning I have relationships, keep in touch, and visit. I was always the niece you would find "up under" you, always being taking somewhere, and always wanting to know what was going on. As a small child, I was in everyone's business and paid attention to every conversation that my little ears could manage to hear. (laughs)

When I think about "character," what comes to mind are a few individuals. The first would be my bonus grandparents, which were really my grandaunt, Nancy Manigault, and my granduncle, Reverend David Manigault. My grandaunt was my maternal grandmother's sister, and my granduncle was my maternal grandfather's brother. I was very close to them and spent a lot of weekends at their house when I was younger.

It was always great going to their house because they had an actual "house." We were from the projects and lived on the twentieth floor of a set of buildings on the infamous Webster Avenue in Bronx, New York. I loved going to their house where there was carpet, steps, an attic, and a basement. Thanksgiving over there would be like an amusement park for me and my cousins. We had so many beautiful memories in that house.

We would sit and have dinner together and talk, and they always taught me lessons and gave me wisdom even at a young age. What I adored was their engagement and relating to each other. It was loving, respectful, consistent, and it WAS GOD. They were the same ALL THE TIME. Their character was on display and I didn't even know what I was really looking at when I was living it, but they were showing me how to live a sanctified life 24/7. It wasn't a Sunday service display, they were really that way. Giving, interceding for others, serving others, going to charities and people's homes to minister, and they made their home a safe haven for worship.

In addition to them, one of my aunts I lived with gave her life to the Lord when I was very small, and I remembered watching her go through changes of growth and maturity. I knew her before Christ, and she herself was young at the time, but when she gave her life to the Lord there became something different about her. A transformation had taken place within her and I was privileged to see her live for Jesus every day of the week, not just on Sundays.

My final example would be my mother. In which she has lived a yielded life before the Lord, and made it her business to teach me and my siblings about Jesus. I actually learned intercession from my mother and the power of prayer from watching her over the years maintain a posture of prayer before the Lord.

Each of these particular family members taught me that living for the Lord was more than a service but it was a lifestyle of worship that was most honorable and integral before the Lord. That we showed the Lord we loved Him by our obedience and surrender, not just our words. I'm grateful for each of them because they taught me the foundation of what I learned later: Integrity leads to good character.

Integrity...

Building with integrity will be the base of your infrastructure. Integrity comes when there is a decision to do right and be right regardless of the circumstance. You could have every right to possibly not do the right thing but feel convicted and compelled to do the right thing anyway. The right thing when no one is looking is going to be just between you and God. You don't want to get so caught up into what others think, but you should always care about how the Lord sees what you are doing.

Who you are behind closed doors and/or in situations where you can't be seen or monitored is where integrity grows. It's when your appetite begins to change and your desires align with God's desires for you. The conviction you carry will position you and you will have the capacity to do what's right when needed. Being a person of integrity makes you trustworthy and dependable, your words have weight and your moral stance is steadfast. To be strong integrally you should review your value system, your beliefs, and your convictions.

Maturity...

Mature builders are effective builders. How you respond, behave, and act toward life happenstances lets you and everyone else know your level of maturity. When things happen unexpectedly, when disappointment occurs, when accidents happen, when plans don't go as planned, and when someone hurts you. How do you respond?

Is it an outburst? With anger? Do you tell people about themselves? Do you have a nasty disposition and forget that you represent the kingdom? Do you use foul language? Do you do "tit for tat"? Are you petty in nature by making small things big things? Do you lie? Do you retaliate? Do you take an opportunity for revenge?

Honest questions require honest answers. Think about it and see where you are, because in order to build, maturity is a must. It will impact your relationships and your ability to collaborate. As a builder, you have to be able to take correction, be rebuked, and be reprimanded by trusted sources. Maturity is needed to navigate some of the natural reflex emotions that come with this part of the building process.

Be self-aware and pay attention to those internal rise ups and inflections in your soul that come up when someone rubs you the wrong way. Remember, even if you respond right on the outside, the Lord knows your heart, so if not-so-good thoughts and feelings come up, and STAY, you want to lay that on the altar. You don't want to build with an orphan spirit and it becomes a harder job to lift in the building when you are oppressed by rejection. Give your heart to the Lord as a builder and let Him heal those secret places so that you can be mature in your mental, emotional, and spiritual capacity.

Good Character...

Some years ago I worked for an organization in a small office with only three additional coworkers. We were a small group and spent a lot of time together, but there was one I didn't care for too much for various reasons. She annoyed me and got under my skin so bad. I felt she was anal and over the top. But again, we were a small group so I almost have what they would have called a "love-hate" relationship with her, which I don't at all feel is acceptable today.

Well, there was a work incident that came up, and I felt that her behavior about that situation was sneaky and there was an intention to get myself and the other coworker in trouble. So, I stopped speaking to her. I would ignore her and speak to her on a need-to basis. If not work related, I would not respond to her at all. This went on for months.

Now, a mini back story with me is that I struggled with unforgiveness BAD. I really did hate people for a long time and would hold grudges for what seemed to feel like forever. I did this to protect myself from being hurt, as I was so many times over the years, but what I didn't know back then was that blocking out people and cutting them off was not only hardening my heart, but it was keeping the Holy Spirit out along with them.

Did I mention this work environment was a Christian organization in which I was proud to actually be a believer working there? Here goes the on-fire-for-God Christian lady that doesn't speak and is mean, smh. It was horrible, but you know what, I felt no conviction about it at that time. I felt merited in my behavior toward her and had no intentions to befriend her.

In the midst of this the job, I joined a new church, and one of the things I loved most about my new church was the purity of heart of my pastor. The church was brand new and he was fresh out the gate into being a senior leader in ministry. His perspective was fresh, it was new, and it was authentic. I related to him quickly because he was so genuine. He even gave me a relaxed posture in church, where prior to that I was somewhat guarded due to some of the things I endured in church.

After sitting under his leadership and teaching for about three to four months, something miraculous happened. One morning I went to work like normal, and that coworker I wasn't fond of said "Good Morning" and I said it back for the first time in months. (Shocked faces on everyone, to include me.) I quickly went to my desk to get settled, and she was so stunned that she followed me to my desk and stood in the doorway of my office. She then attempts small talk to keep the conversation going, and I cut it short. In my head, I'm like lady, baby steps, baby steps. I'm being worked on. (Laughing out loud)

I never not spoke to her again. I realized over the next few days to weeks one of the main reasons the Lord sent me to that ministry, it wasn't just to help build ... it was for Him to work on my heart to fix my character. At that time I could prophesy, corporately pray, evangelize, minister deliverance, sing worship, dance worship, and actively flow in my gifts. But, NONE of that meant anything with bad character and a bad attitude.

Although I loved when my cousins joined me, my visits were the most impactful when I stayed with them by myself. I would wake up to worship in the morning, my aunt singing in the kitchen while cooking, or her singing in her family room while sewing. My uncle was usually watching a football game in their living room, or in the basement family room recording his practice sermons in the pulpit.

It doesn't matter how endowed you are with gifts, if the container that is housing those gifts is a dirty vessel, meaning the character, integrity, and heart currents are questionable, none of that holds weight long term. It's not okay to carry ourselves in a manner that compromises our intimacy with Holy Spirit and to misrepresent the Father. You never know whom is watching and when the Lord may need you to be available. That same coworker, after months of rebuilding some type of professional rapport with her, I was able to help her with a work crisis she encountered. In which she was grateful for, because that circumstance would have impacted our organization greatly. What was most precious to me was that when she eventually resigned from her job a few months after that, I was able to pray for her, minister Jesus and deliverance to her in that office before she left. We both cried, hugged each other, and she left. I never saw her again, but I was grateful that I was able to be on post and didn't miss an opportunity to be His hands and feet because my character wasn't in check.

Bad character has to do with your attitude, disposition, integrity, what you think is right and wrong, your life choices and decisions, how you treat people, how you respond to responsibility, your true heart motives, and the fibers of your personality. Character takes you a long way, and the best of builders are the ones with the conviction of good character.

Chapter 3

Lead in Grace

In 2018 I was given my first official leadership role, one role in the community and the other in church. Both of these roles began within sixty days of each other, and I had no idea what I was doing in both instances. I wasn't provided a road map or blueprint of what to do, how to manage teams, and how to develop them. Both organizations were fairly new in their current state, so it was up to me to create something that didn't exist. Everything I did was literally led and guided by Holy Spirit. I leaned on Him because I had no choice, but it was the best thing I could have done.

Prior to that year, I would have never considered myself a leader, it wasn't even something that I gave attention to or strived toward. Even when given the responsibility my thoughts were, okay, so I am responsible for some things? Okay, cool ... but it didn't dawn on me that I was an actual leader. I always came up with ideas and thought of ways to do things better, but that never correlated. I ignored my leadership qualities and abilities for years. Although I often didn't feel worthy, I knew it was inevitable due to what God allowed me to endure the years before.

I was being prepared and positioned, and although eventually I knew it would come, it was all still overwhelming when the opportunities sought me out. There were days I cried, days I felt stuck, and days I was suffering, but I was so honored by the responsibility of being assigned to a leadership role that I didn't let that interfere with my leading. During the first year of my leadership, I endured four close family deaths, lost two friendships, and my teenage daughter hit a downhill spiral of depression. It was an extremely trying time for me, trying to manage it all. I was extremely emotional and endured a crash course on how to lead with consistency, integrity, and faithfulness despite how I felt.

I experienced some of the most humbling and touching experiences of my life. In these roles, I grew relationships with those I was leading, and they became my family. I feel I need to mention that these men and women were not just any individuals, but some of the most gifted men and women that I have ever had the privilege to know and do life with. They will always be special to me, and many of them are in the chapters to come. I share that because it should be said that I had to get past being intimidated by what I couldn't do or who I wasn't. I had to address my insecurities head on so that I would not project any of my shortcomings on them and could lead them "fairly."

As the leader, you are held in a different esteem, a higher regard, and responsibility. They were precious cargo and belonged to the Lord. He entrusted me with their giftings, so I was going to make Him proud and love on them. I took my responsibility too seriously to handle God's people recklessly because of my personal challenges. I was very serious about my assignment.

By God's grace, I was able to man my post and lead effectively that whole year. It was a challenge, but I can honestly say it does grow easier over time to lead and feel strong, not lead in fear. There will always be obstacles at any and every stage or level of your leadership journey. However, if you stay consistent and accountable you will gain knowledge and wisdom to be able to maneuver and navigate each season gracefully.

There were a few things I learned as a leader that I would like to share with you because leading is a major part of the building process. You may be building the "thing," but you, the leader, are housing the vision, so being a good leader is a focal point. If you do all the internal work mentioned in these previous chapters, it leads you here.

Leadership 101

As a leader, I have learned and implemented:

- You must be a person of vision. You can't expect people to follow you or trust you without clarity of where everyone is going and where you are leading them to.

- You must be humble. He opposes the proud but gives grace to the humble (James 4:6).

- Remember as the overseer, you are serving them, it's not the other way around.

- Take time to know your team. As a leader I have built personable individual relationships with each and every person I lead. When we come together collaboratively it helps with our unity. It also builds rapport between me and them.

- Cultivate their giftings. When you take the time to get to know the team you can identify strengths and weaknesses. You need to know that so you know how to position them.

- Determine new and fresh ways to keep them motivated, inspired, and focused on the goal.

- Don't just dictate but delegate. Dictating is giving orders with no direction while delegating should come with a form of training on the "how to." Because you have been cultivating the team, delegating tasks to them in the building process gives them muscles and stamina.

- Duplicate yourself. The success of a leader is the leaders they help groom that they serve. Help them achieve their personal goals OUTSIDE of the collaborative work that is being done on that team.

- Be honest and forthcoming with them.

- PRAY FOR THEM as individuals for their personal lives, not just as the people on the team. Make time to minister to them as well.

Compassion...

Some of the best leaders I have been under carried the component of compassion, they were selfless and understood the meaning of sacrifice.

When you show genuine care and concern for where others are, you will be amazed on how they come through for you, and how they are dedicated and committed to the work of the build. Having compassion creates a safe place for those you build with, it shows them you are concerned, and it gives them an opportunity for you to help with some of their distress. Being empathetic is great, but if you can actually "do" something to help them, you should. The body of Christ, we the church are the world's solution. When there is something within our power to do to help, we need to.

The love of Christ covers a multitude and all we do should convey His love. You must have a soft heart and remember not only that it could be you, but that one day IT WILL be you on the receiving end. Treat everyone simply the way you would want to be treated.

As a leader you are an intercessor for those you lead, you will cover them and stand in the gap for them. Leaders build people, projects, and infrastructures. They organize, oversee, and facilitate. They understand that the vision is great so they don't try to do it alone, but they actively sharpen every member of their team to ensure the firm strength of the build-out. They are kingdom focused and are intentional about their growth, their development, and their healing.

Whether you are a leader in your ministry, church, job, organization, home, or community group ... lead with honor in His name and with His character.

ARCHITECTS

| Elouise Townsend |

| Luis Trochez |

| Lakia Perez |

| Justin Goodman |

| Ciara Mason |

| Dr. Chavon Anette |

| Gary Ellick |

| Dr. Charlene D Winley |

| Robert Bennett Jr |

| Erica Ojada |

| Andre Mason |

Authentic Leadership

by Elouise Townsend[3]

By the time you realize what it is you want to do, you then realize you've already been doing it in an informal capacity.

Our natural ability is innate and we sometimes don't identify it right off the bat because it's so entwined with our natural personality. Therefore, we don't see it as a gift or talent, we just say, "That's me." Yes, that is you, the you that the world needs to encounter as soon as you take a step toward them, so they can see the value of the God-given gifts and talents you have to offer.

For eighteen years, I worked in corporate America in the wireless communications industry. I started out just wanting a job so I would have something to do once my two youngest children started school. I worked part time but went in five days a week when I started. On my third day of my new job, I was left alone to close the location where I worked. My coworker grabbed his keys and his coat and said goodnight. I didn't say it out loud, but I thought, *where is he going?* Then, I realized they'd decided to just leave me alone to figure out what to do. I believe my coworker's attitude was, they hired her, and they have to train her. I'm out!

After a couple of minutes of realizing that I was left to do a job that I was clueless about, I decided to take on the attitude of, oh well, they left me here. I'm going to do what I can and if I mess up, that's their fault.

When the next customer walked up to the kiosk, I thought, *ok, you can do this. Just talk to the people and see what they want.*

As days, weeks, and months went by, I never forgot my first encounter with the customer I serviced. They had no idea I was clueless about my job. The customers I helped couldn't see my lack of knowledge of the industry because I just talked to them. I just had a conversation with them to see what they wanted and geared them toward their desires.

Within a year of me starting with my new company, they promoted me to supervisor and made me full time. I became more and more comfortable with just talking to people and listening to their needs, wants, frustrations, and anything else that was thrown at me. Not all in a bad way. I realized that my customers didn't talk to me because I was a great salesperson, I recognized that they talked to me because they trusted me. Over time, it wasn't just the customers who freely and comfortably talked to me, it was also my coworkers.

It wasn't long before I understood very clearly that the key to a genuine, solid, and respectful relationship in the workplace was just simply to be myself. If I'm just myself, I can just relax and flow from an authentic place. People can see and feel you in that space, and it is there where you are trusted. As much as I saw people around me pretend to be someone they were not in the industry I worked in, you know, just to get a sale, I could never be anyone other than who I was. No pretense, no added agenda. What you say out of your mouth is your heart's intent. For me, it is that old adage of what you see is what you get.

You may wonder how to stay authentic in the workplace and as a leader. Won't I be too vulnerable? Or appear as a pushover? Won't my possible transparency lead people to think that they can take advantage of me? Those are good questions. Authenticity doesn't mean total transparency; it means your integrity is on constant display. It means your words are as good as gold and your words and actions align.

When you are authentic, or as we may say, "real," people identify with that immediately. They see that you are moving freely and confidently in your speech and in your ways. These actions make people comfortable and they are prompted to be as open and authentic as you are. They trust what they hear and see, so they put down their guard in response to your authentic nature.

Authenticity leads to consistency, consistency leads to productivity, and productivity leads to a thriving business or organization.

It is up to every leader as to what kind of standard they want to set in their workplace, organization, and their own business. As you set your initial standards, understand that this is the environment that you will be creating, organizing, and building in.

When you as a leader are consistent, the people you are leading will trust you and they will get to know you and what you expect from them without wondering. Consistency destroys ambiguity, so communication and expectations become clear.

In most cases, what you establish as a leader will function the way you envisioned it, as long as clear and concise goals and expectations are laid out in the very beginning. Unfortunately, you will almost always be challenged with that one person that may have seen eye to eye with you in the beginning, but somewhere along the line, their vision changed. That person will challenge your ability to lead or to communicate your thoughts and ideas properly. This can be very frustrating for any leader. Resolving this issue has to be handled somewhat delicately. Handling an unruly team member while keeping your standards intact and making a fair and just determination on how to resolve the issue is key. Understand that you are being watched by the whole team. So, they are looking to see if you are still going to hold on to your word. They will be looking to see your tolerance level with someone who disrespectfully does not line up with your vision. This may be very challenging, but here is an opportunity to confirm and solidify the original goal and expectation, not just for your unruly team member, but also for the others that will definitely be watching to see your response. As a leader, this will be one of your most stressful times while leading people. Although you may have to discipline one person, everything you've ever told your team and everything you've ever shown your team will be on display in your response. Only you know what's best for you your team, your organization, or your workplace.

Remember, authenticity is consistency, and consistency filters into every area of your leadership.

The Blueprint

by Luis Trochez[4]

UNLESS *the* **Lord builds** *the house,* they **labor in vain** *who build it;*
UNLESS *the* **Lord Guards** *the city, The watchman* **stays awake in vain.**
Psalm 127:1 (NJKV)

There are two kinds of people: a wise person and a foolish person. Which one are you? One who labors in vain and one who labors in purpose. Again, I ask, "Which one are you?" Most of us will immediately respond, "Of course, I'm the wise one! No question about it!" Where I would reply, to human standards you may be correct, but to God's standards we are far off—"There is a way that seems right to a man, But its end is the way of death (destruction)" (*Proverbs 14:12 NKJV*). "There is a generation that is pure in its own eyes, Yet is not washed from its filthiness" (*Proverbs 30:12 NKJV*).

So, the question now is, "How do we become wise and build or labor in purpose?" For that we must turn to the Master Builder—Our Heavenly Father (the Source of all things). Our Lord Jesus says it best in *Matthew 7:24–27 (ESV)*.

Build Your House on the Rock
[24] "Everyone then who hears these words of mine and does them will be like a wise man who built his house on the rock.

> [25] *And the rain fell, and the floods came, and the winds blew and beat on that house, but it did not fall, because it had been founded on the rock.* [26] *And everyone who hears these words of mine and does not do them will be like a foolish man who built his house on the sand.* [27] *And the rain fell, and the floods came, and the winds blew and beat against that house, and it fell, and great was the fall of it."*

I would like to quickly point your attention to a few key elements from this verse of scripture that I believe will make you a Great Builder, no matter what you are building—whether it be a relationship with God, building a marriage, starting a family, building a career, a business, a ministry, or raising children:

1. A wise man hears the words spoken by the Father and does them.

2. A foolish man also hears the words spoken by the Father and does them—NOT.

3. Calamity strikes both a wise man and a foolish man—it doesn't discriminate.

4. A wise man endures the tests and trials—they persevere, whereas a foolish man encounters great destruction when the tests and trials strike.

5. Divine instructions are given to both, BUT a wise man obeys and a foolish man disobeys.

Proverbs 9:10 (NKJV), "**The fear of the Lord** is the beginning of **wisdom**, And the **knowledge** of the **Holy One** is **understanding**."

I want to highlight something important. If your desire is not to be a "one-hit wonder," but rather leave an everlasting impact and an inheritance to your children's, children's, children, then the Foundation to what you are building MUST be founded or rooted on a material and substance that can last the test of time, or else it'll be foolishness for you to start building. Whatever we build in our own wisdom and understanding eventually crumbles, but what is built in God's Wisdom and Understanding endures forever.

> Luke 14:28-29 (NKJV)
> [28] For which of you, intending to build a tower, does not sit down first and count the cost, whether he has enough to finish it— [29] lest, after he has laid the foundation, and is not able to finish, all who see it begin to mock him,

> Zechariah 4:6 (NKJV emphasized)
> [6] So he answered and said to me:
> "This is the word of the Lord to Zerubbabel:
> 'Not by [your] might nor by [your] power, but by My Spirit,'
> Says the Lord of hosts.

Let's meditate on these words from our opening scripture, *"UNLESS the Lord builds..., UNLESS the Lord guards (Shamar)..."* Seeking God's wisdom and His Protection is mandatory when it comes to building—ANYTHING. Having a desire, zeal, and skillset is NOT enough. All these things are good, but what will make you wise or foolish is solely being empowered and led by His Wisdom, His Might, His Strength, and His Spirit. Then and only then will you receive another KEY component, which is vastly overlooked but imperative to the successful establishment of your "Architecture." No wise Architect begins building without first planning, designing, and counting the cost *(Luke 14:28-31)*. A wise Architect understands that "the Blueprint" is essential to the success of his building. A foolish Architect takes shortcuts, but the wise seek Counsel in the developing of this Blueprint. I will say it again, "It's not by your counsel but by His Spirit (His Counsel)—says the Lord."

In this age of obsession over instant success, I'm led to give you a word of warning; don't be fooled by the success of other foolish builders. Always remember, "There is a way that seems right to a man, but its end is the way of death (destruction)" *(Proverbs 14:12)*. "So Pursue God's [Keys of] Wisdom and Protections at all times and Obey His Blueprint (Instructions), then the Power to Create Wealth is Unlocked" *(Deuteronomy 8:18)*.

What I've come to understand is we all inherit a Blueprint to either build something new or a Blueprint to rebuild something anew. For some of you, like Solomon, the Blueprint was handed to you by your father, and you are trying to build the legacy that your father and your forefathers started but were unsuccessful. Not because they didn't have the zeal, the desire, and motivations, but simply because their assignment was just to develop the Blueprint and pass it on to you so that you can build the legacy. And as you build, your children will receive the inheritance of what you are building. King David did not see with his physical eyes the Temple of the Lord in all its glory, but I'm sure he did see it with his spiritual eyes as the Blueprint was given to him by God.

For those of us who have inherited the Blueprint to Build something anew, this Blueprint comes with its own set of special instructions. Is one Blueprint more valuable than the other? ABSOLUTELY NOT! Both carry the essence of Heaven and are given by God to His Children. The Blueprint to rebuild is given to those of us whom our Father has Graced and marked with what I call, **"the Jeremiah 1:10 Grace."**

> *¹⁰ See, I have this day set you over the nations and over the kingdoms,*
> *To root out and to pull down,*
> *To destroy and to throw down,*
> *To build and to plant."*

These "Jeremiah 1:10 Architects" are Graced to first dismantle, demolish, and destroy the nations, kingdoms, and systems that have enslaved and oppressed God's children with misery, lack, failure, bondage, setback, addictions, destruction, and poverty. Such are to be first rooted out, pulled down, destroyed, and overthrown to make way for the Foundation of Rock, which is in Christ. After the

"Jeremiah 1:10 Architect" has uprooted, destroyed, torn down, and removed, then he can build and he can plant that which has been ordained by God.

> *Ezekiel 22:30 (Expanded Bible)*
> *30 "I looked for someone to ·build up [repair; Ezekiel 13:5] the walls and to stand before me ·where the walls are broken [in the gap/breach] ·to defend these people [on behalf of the land] so I would not have to destroy them. But I could not find anyone.*

Will the Lord of Hosts find you in the path of submission to His Will? In that place where the Blueprint to Build according to His Will is released? Will the Lord find a wise heart? Or a foolish heart?

The Blueprint

Graced for It

by Lakia Perez[5]

The best way to start this chapter would have to be with this thought, "Only what you do for Christ will last." This idea comes from 2 Corinthians 5:9-10 (CSB), which states, "Therefore, whether we are at home or away, we make it our aim to be pleasing to him. For we must all appear before the judgment seat of Christ, so that each may be repaid for what he has done in body, whether good or evil." This text encourages us as Kingdom builders to focus on pleasing the Lord in everything. As a creative, marketplace planter, and ministry builder, it's important to understand that everyone is not graced to do what you are called to do. This is why it's important to keep your ear pressed to the Father's lips.

Let me take you on my journey as a Kingdom Builder. My name is Lakia Perez, I am a forty-seven-year-old lover of Jesus. I am a Retired Navy Veteran with two men that God blessed me with: Noel, 27, and Donaven, 23. I am the leader of Women of Life Ministries since 2010 and the owner of Christian Life Radio Station since 2017. Ministry and Entrepreneurship is not for the faint at heart. This is why it is important that you are in the will of the Father. When you are in the will of the Father, there is grace to execute and build. That does not mean it will be easy, but amid chaos, grace covers. When you are weary, grace will get you through. When you must deal with difficult people, grace will sustain you. In this chapter, I will focus on three areas: Identity, Development, and Resilience.

When building in the marketplace, it's important to know who you are. When God gives you vision to build, it's given to you based on your unique makeup in which He created you. This is why you may see many businesses that are the same, but they differ in identity and the functionality of the business. So, embrace your authenticity because that is where the oil of God will flow from. In 2017, I launched the radio station, but along the way, stopped and needed to regroup. I heard God say, "Relaunch Christian Life Radio," so I did in 2020 out of obedience. This was during the pandemic, when everyone was launching a podcast or radio station. I began to feel like what I was doing was not much compared to what others were doing. I had to understand that I was not only rejecting me, but I was rejecting the God genius that He created me with.

The Word declares, "Let us make man in our image." Those lies of the enemy were hindering me from flowing out of the image I was created in. In order to stay true to your unique self, you must stay near the Father. John 15:5-6 reminds us, "Remain in Me, and I will remain in you. Just as no branch can bear fruit by itself unless it remains in the vine, neither can you bear fruit unless you remain in Me. I am the vine and you are the branches. The one who remains in Me, and I in him, will bear much fruit. For apart from Me you can do nothing." This text helps me understand that as I abide in the Father, it will keep me secure in who I am because He made me. It will keep me true to the vision He gave me and so that I am not doing what everybody else is doing. Remember that there is only one you, and the real you is needed. So, stay in your lane.

Let us talk about this development process. It is not always a wonderful process, but it is good for you. When I relaunched the station, I did not know much about running a station and I am still growing. I want to share this analogy with you that the Lord shared with me during my quiet time. When someone has a baby for the first time, it is scary because they have never mothered. However, what happens is that brand-new mother will grow with the baby. For example, when the baby cries, the mother will see if the baby is hungry, tired, or irritated by something. This is the time where the mom and baby are familiarizing themselves with one another. As the baby is growing, so is she. She is learning how to be a mother in the act of being one. Just the same in business, we must treat it like a brand-new baby and grow with it. You will make good choices and bad choices, but you are learning, growing, and maturing through it all. This process will equip and fortify you. Then, you will be able to see from experience what changes need to be made or if you just need to start over, like I did, and that is OKAY! So, allow this scripture to bless you as you grow with your baby, "Therefore, my beloved brothers, be steadfast, immovable, always abounding in the work of the Lord, knowing that in the Lord your labor is not in vain" (1 Corinthians 15:58).

As you are being built in the development process, it positions you as a Kingdom Builder who holds his or her ground in the marketplace. This is the next key, resilience. Resilience is one who recovers quickly from a strong hit, one who has the capacity to withstand every attack that comes their way. These attacks will manifest in many ways like the mind, emotions, physical body, finances, your family, marriage, or whatever is dear to your heart. The enemy cannot stand God's Kingdom agenda being expanded, so he will do what he can by placing snares in your way to frustrate, irritate, and destroy you. The word reminds us of this in John 10:10, "The thief comes only to steal and kill and destroy; I have come that they may have life and have it to the full." Although warfare may be great, remember that you are built for this. God has created you to overcome and finish what He has placed in you because He promised in Philippians 1:6, "I am convinced *and* confident of this very thing, that He who has begun a good work in you will [continue to] perfect *and* complete it until the day of Christ Jesus [the time of His return]." This is what I learned as I walked with the Lord during this journey; that I can do all things through Christ who strengthens me. Through the Holy Spirit, He will lead me, encourage, comfort me, teach me, and reveal the truth to me.

So, as I close out this chapter, I encourage you to be strong in the Lord and in the Power of His might. The reason you are reading this right now is evident you have been called to build. So, build. Remember to write the vision and make it plain; seek God for instructions and wisdom; keep your ears pressed to his lips; allow the Holy Spirit to be your guide, teacher, and comforter. Most importantly, make sure what you do pleases God. So, I leave you with this thought, "It's not what you're doing for God that matters, but it's that you're doing it for Him that does!"

Two Left Feet

by Justin Goodman[6]

Get up offa that thing, and dance 'til you feel better- James Brown

James Brown is known as the Godfather of Soul! Born on May 3, 1933, he became a prominent worldwide performer and pioneered what we call funk music. He helped develop and impacted several different genres of music throughout his fifty-year career. Unfortunately, he died on Christmas Day in 2006. However, his music and legacy lives on 'til this day. One of his most famous songs is called "Get Up Offa That Thing." This is simply a song that is designed to make you DANCE. The lyrics are all about you getting up and dancing until you feel better. One of the lines is, "Get up offa that thing and try to release that pressure!" In my opinion, this is a golden nugget in the context of being a builder. One of the keys of building successfully is learning how to dance between the tension that building creates. Some people fail to successfully build organizations, businesses, and brands because they refuse to DANCE. What do I mean by dance? I am using the idea of dancing figuratively in order to communicate the concept of balancing all that is involved when building.

I am one that cannot literally dance. I make a fool of myself every time I attempt to "cut a step" at a social gathering. I am told that I have "two left feet." Nevertheless, because I have been blessed with the ability to move, I dance anyway. This chapter is not about us being skilled, equipped, talented, or even gifted to dance or build. It is to encourage you to get up and dance anyway, even if you don't know what you're doing all the time.

One of my favorite quotes is from Thomas Edison, which says, "I have not failed. I've just found 10,000 ways that won't work." This hits home with me because I can identify that through my years of building my business and life itself, I've attempted so many things to better my situations; some worked, and many didn't. It seems contrary because I come from a long lineage of business owners. My great-grandparents owned a gas station, grocery store, barbershop, and a cafe, all in the segregated South in the early 1900s. My maternal grandparents owned a wedding and decor business. My fraternal grandparents owned a charter bus company and pony riding business. My father is a serial entrepreneur and he currently owns a septic tank service. My mother started a homecare agency in 2013, which I co-own with her. To say that entrepreneurship is in my blood is an understatement. However, even though my history is filled with the precious legacy of entrepreneurship, the knowledge and wisdom of being my own boss was not translated with the DNA.

Some people who do not come from families of business owners may disqualify themselves. They may feel that they lack key ingredients that make up entrepreneurs. One of the biggest disqualifications I've heard someone say is that they did not come from a business-oriented family. It is true that business owners, entrepreneurs, and builders have a unique DNA. I wholeheartedly believe that we are wired differently. However, I do not believe you had to have come from the right environment to be a great builder. I want to expose the lie that just because you were not raised in the environment of successful entrepreneurs means you can't become one. You can become anything you want to be. I am a testament of this! Like I mentioned earlier, my family is stocked with business owners. Nevertheless, I have learned that it takes grit, wisdom, humility, and learning to dance in the tension to be a successful builder, no matter what's in your blood.

I have discovered that a key part in dancing is learning how to pivot. Wikipedia defines it like this, "In dance, a pivot turn is a general classification for dance turns in which the performer's body rotates about its vertical axis without traveling." Whether hip-hop dances, line dances, or ballroom dances, pivots are core. If you learn how to pivot, you can dance. Some pivots are not as polished as others, but the important thing is that the pivot happens. Personally, the line dance "Wobble" gets me caught up every time. That pivot is dangerous to one like myself who has two left feet. Even so, I still attempt and successfully turn around, no matter how ugly it is! As time gets better, I get better at my pivots. I practice my pivots.

Practicing pivots should be a habitual behavior for any builder. As James Brown said, "Try to release that pressure." The only way you can release the pressures building creates is pivoting from what may not be working anymore. As a builder, you cannot afford to romanticize one way of doing things. You have to do what the season requires of you. I personally don't believe in the work-life balance concept. Some seasons require more work and some may require more life investment. I lean more to the school of thought where we should find the rhythm vs finding the balance. I don't think we should strive to find the perfect measure of work and life. In essence, we build by learning how to dance in the tension!

Years ago, in my journey to building my homecare agency, I learned this concept of dancing in the tension. There were many times I had to pivot, along with our system operations. Homecare is a very unique industry. You have to care for individual clients in their homes. You also have to manage employees and aides. And lastly, you must stay in compliance with state and federal regulations. It is tough! Especially, if you are in the process of building clientele. There was one season in our business where my mother and I went on an aggressive marketing campaign. By the grace of God, we went from averaging eleven clients to about thirty. Thirty clients is a fairly large client base. Due to this increase, we had to change our operations and systems because the current way we were doing things could not withstand the growth. The biggest thing we needed was more aides, specifically fill-in aides. You see, when an aide calls out, we can't afford to have no one show up, especially if the client has no one home to care for them. That means our workforce needed extra nurses to send in times of emergencies. With double the clientele, we needed double the aides and fill-in staff. The issue we were having was a lack of fill-in staff. My mother and I were literally taking the few staffers we had from one job to another several times a day. It was becoming exhausting. What was a light, kind gesture when we were at eleven clients became a horrific burden at thirty clients. We had to decide, either stay small as a company and keep our operations the same, or pivot and create new ways of doing things.

We were successful at growing the business. The grind it took to grow our business was not the same behavior needed to actually sustain the growth. We decided to change our intake procedures and slow down the process of starting new cases. In this season, we had to pivot at least three major times. Our first pivot was deciding to grow the company. We could have either stayed comfortable, or did what we did, grow! There was a lot of tension in that. Tension of sacrificing time and energy to invest in the business. We had to deal with the tension of some team members not wanting to add tasks to their daily routines. The tensions were there! These new tensions did not come with a reference book. We had to simply "get up offa that thing" and learn the new rhythm of our company until the tension was released.

The next pivot was within the building process. In our growing phase, we had to make several pivots. In that season, I determined the necessity of the pivots by determining if our methods were net positives for the company. A net positive approach is to basically make sure that holistically you are receiving more in value, money, time, peace, and energy than you are putting out. After all your efforts are done and the building is complete, if you get less value, money, time, peace, and energy, especially in business, you are in the net negative.

In the season of us building up our clientele, it was ok for us to pull long hours for a few months because we were building something.

The holistic picture was coming together. Some people would argue that it's not healthy to be unbalanced in work. My perspective is when you are building, as long as the holistic picture will yield net-positive results, I think it's ok.

The final pivot we did in that season was to pivot from building, to sustaining what was built. New tension was created after the building was complete. What was a net positive in one season began to seep toward the net-negative meter. Again, we had to dance in the tension. We had to "get up offa that thing to try to release that pressure." We had to find a new rhythm for the new season.

As you work toward building whatever it is you're building, remember that it's a marathon, not a sprint. There will be growing pains, frustrations, and confusion. One of the most important keys is to not stay in a place that's not producing. If you lack production, you will feel defeated. Builders feel really bad when nothing is being built. You may have to pivot! Get up offa that thing and BUILD!!!!

Jumping the Hurdles of Opposition

by Ciara Mason[7]

As I sat down to brainstorm the focus and takeaways I desired every builder to gain from this chapter, I immediately saw a warning sign. Now, we all know that warning signs are set up to indicate a potential hazard, obstacle, or condition that would require special attention from those in the vicinity. Even as construction workers have dozens of warning and caution signs plastered around the work site, we as builders must be aware of the caution signs around us. Here's a major one...

WARNING: YOUR DECISION TO BUILD WILL MAKE YOU A TARGET FOR OPPOSITION.

Now, this chapter is in no way meant to deter you from building. The sole reason for my sharing of experiences and the wisdom gained is to ensure that builders can identify the hurdles of opposition and subsequently leap over them. So, take a moment to stretch because we're about to leap!

MY STORY

In the winter of 2018, I received the instruction to start a small Facebook group for women. Nothing major, or so I thought. I foresaw inviting a few women with a similar passion for God to join me for prayer meetings, bible studies, and fellowships every now and then. I knew how valuable being a part of a tribe was to women, especially in my age group, and I could see the need/desire for it. So, although I was quite afraid and honestly didn't feel fully equipped, I gave God my "yes" and set my heart to move forward with the assignment.

On February 11, 2019, I created the Razing Women group. I can't tell you how excited I was. While still unsure of how this would go, I knew I was going with God, and that was enough. Spoiler alert: Over the course of three years, my small idea has exploded into a multigenerational, multicultural tribe of 3,000+ women from across the United States and abroad. We gather weekly for corporate prayer, bi-weekly for bible study, and even host a sought-after annual conference. Only God could do this! What I saw as "small," God called great.

THE OPPOSITION

Looking back on it, I believe I came to the awareness of the group's greatness at the same time the enemy did. Toward the end of year two, as our membership and impact were surging, behind the scene all hell was breaking loose and I was contemplating shutting it all down.

What happened? The hurdle of opposition was thrown out in front of me, mid race. I was blindsided by lies, slander, and harsh criticism. Out of the blue, I was made aware of drastic false truths that were being said about me, as a leader. My morals and motives were being questioned. The crazy part was, I couldn't identify the source of the confusion in a line-up. I had no clue who the culprit was. You would think this detail would make the incident one that was easy to shake off. Wrong! I cried for days! I was tormented by the lies at the most random times of the day. I didn't want to pray or teach. I didn't trust anyone. I continually questioned how someone could think so little of me. Could they not see my heart? My only objective was to obey God and build a community of strong women warriors. I was giving it my all, requiring nothing from others. Why am I facing opposition?

"Because you're building something significant," God gently responded.

Only a naive person would expect to build something of significance without ever facing some form of opposition. While mine came through slander, yours could be dressed as financial woes, loss of support, legal trouble, health issues, etc. Regardless, they are all the same, HURDLES. The choice is the same for each of us. Will you allow this hurdle to stop you from running? Or will you make up your mind to leap over it?

After my days of crying, pity parties, and threatening to quit, the Lord spoke to my heart and let me know that what I deemed as small was a huge threat to the enemy. My perspective was skewed and it needed to be adjusted quickly. This work was bigger than me, just as your work is so much bigger than you.

Pause, lay your hand on your chest, and say, "THIS WORK IS BIGGER THAN ME." Take that in. *(Selah)*

THE GAME CHANGER

Armed with the worth of my life's work, I began to rebuild. Being a builder that is also a believer, it only seemed right to turn to the word of God for my rebuilding strategy. God, in his wisdom, led me to the book of Nehemiah. With each chapter, I felt understood, supported, and empowered to finish the work.

For those who may not be familiar with this book of the Bible, Nehemiah details the rebuilding of the walls of Jerusalem, spearheaded by a man named Nehemiah. This book highlights his burden to build, the favor that was upon him to build, the opposition against his efforts, and ultimately, the success of his building project. Although Nehemiah was doing a great work, a God work, one that benefited many people, he still had to fight against bold opposition. In the thick of his enemies plotting, fighting, and stirring up trouble against him, Nehemiah prayed and then gave those serving with him a three-part instruction that I, too, implemented and found great victory in. If you are facing opposition, I want you to write down these three instructions and put them into action, starting today.

"Then as I looked over the situation, I called together the nobles and the rest of the people and said to them, "Don't be afraid of the enemy! Remember the Lord, who is great and glorious, and fight for your brothers, your sons, your daughters, your wives, and your homes!" Nehemiah 4:14 (NLT)

Instruction #1: DO NOT FEAR

2 Timothy 1:7 states that God has not given us the spirit of fear, but of power and of love and of a sound mind. I know your opposition appears to be more powerful than you are, but they are no match for the one who is with you. Do not fear their words, do not fear their attacks, do not fear failure, nor the verdict. Daily surrender your work back to God and hide in the shelter of His wings. Though a thousand fall at your side, though ten thousand are dying around you, believe that no evil will touch you.

Instruction #2: REMEMBER

On a daily basis, call to mind the one who called you. For the one who called you is faithful and will not fail. Remember the flawless track record of the one who appointed you. Remember that you aren't building for fun but for the benefit of those around you and those to come. Remember you were chosen and equipped by the ultimate builder to accomplish a great work in the earth.

Instruction #3: FIGHT

Lastly, set your mind to fight. This is not a "stand still and see the salvation of the Lord" moment. This victory is going to require your fight. This assignment will require you to grab your divine weapons (2 Corinthians 10:4). Fight for what and who matters. Fight to Finish!

In conclusion, I encourage you to not come down from your work until it is complete. May you find comfort in the words of Colossians 3:23–24, "Whatever you do, work at it with all your heart, as working for the Lord, not for human masters, since you know that you will receive an inheritance from the Lord as a reward. It is the Lord Christ you are serving."

Trust the Architect

by Dr. Chavon Anette[8]

Build – construct (something) by putting parts or materials together. 2020 was indeed a time of putting parts together to build something that I did not have the full blueprint for, but God was saying "go."

Architect – a person who is qualified to design buildings and to plan and supervise their construction. As a builder, our job is to follow the direction of the architect—God. There are times God tells you to build without showing you everything, but you follow the instructions trusting that what is to come of it will be masterful. We must trust God to lead and allow him to be a part of the building from beginning to end.

In 2020, my life changed drastically and quickly. I received instructions from the Lord at the end of 2019 to invite people to a Monday Motivation Moment that I had started to do back in 2018. When the Lord told me to invite others on, I did get nervous because I thought to myself, *What would people have to say? Who does she think she is?* Those, of course, were lies of the enemy. Individuals were eager to share the platform with me when I started interviewing people. However, it was during the pandemic that things started picking up. Instead of interviewing people one time a week, I started interviewing people three times a week. On top of that, I launched my first coaching program as a new certified Life Coach. God truly shot me out like an arrow as things began to shift, speaking engagements started to come, and coaching increased. God was allowing my life to look like what he showed me when I was younger. Then, on top of the interviews and coaching business, the community was launching for leaders.

I started the Power and Grace Leaders Community because I was a leader who often felt out of place and alone as I did things that my family members had not done, nor many people around me. The Lord led me to start a community where leaders could be encouraged, empowered, and educated. It would connect with the doctoral program I started in 2018 at Liberty University. I had no idea of what would come of all these new things God had me doing, but I was indeed building with him. It seemed like in just a few months, by doing the new things God told me to do, my life was shifting in a way I did not expect. As one who always encouraged others, the encouragement and empowerment of others with me was absolutely the foundation of building the Kingdom with God.

Three years later, and God has done more than I could have imagined he would do: Owner of a non-profit, visionary of a best-selling anthology series, leading, speaking on stages I could not have imagined, hosting conferences and events, coaching people out of bondage and into purpose, and so much more. I am not who I was in 2019. I have become and transformed into something only the architect could have seen. Isn't it beautiful that the architect will cause us to build something magnanimous, while also ensuring that the building process makes us into better builders, better people, better disciples, better carriers of the gospel?

However, as a builder, you must know that the journey is not a bed of roses. There are dark times and real challenges you could not have anticipated you would encounter. How do you manage the weight and responsibility to build? You desire to manage your tenacity, momentum, and stamina as you did when you first began. Unfortunately, this fight to stay full throttle on the gas as a builder is dangerous. The pull will cause you to be more focused on the work and not the next set of instructions from the architect. This causes the builder to become unbalanced when there should be balance.

Balance - a condition in which different elements are equal or in the correct proportions. When there is no balance, the strength is in the work rather than the flow.

As Kingdom builders, the strength must always be in the flow of God because we cannot do work ordained by God on human strength. It takes God to do a God assignment. It is through that flow that we can gain wisdom and maturity on how to be a master builder like our father. If not, building without balance causes strain on relationships, physical bodies, mental health, and so much more. While you build, if something happens that afflicts your soul or your body, there must be attention given to that area with God. If not, we preach, prophesy, and pray from the last encounter instead of being refreshed. The danger is that all the energy you are expending is for nothing because we can only get so far on our own. The magnitude of the vision and the joy of purpose comes out of presence. I had to learn this the hard way, needing to take a break from school, my body physically under distress, and mental anguish. However, I came to a place where I had to make time to be still again. I let go of striving, and I removed the idol of success from my heart. I had to get back to the building because the architect chose me to do work that I could only do with him.

Allowing yourself to get off the hamster wheel of the building and instead keeping God at the center of the building brings you to a place of balance. It is there where God ensures the conditions are as they should be, and the proportions are correct. It renews and refreshes the joy of the life of a builder. It does not mean it is without challenges, but it does mean that you will be able to manage the weight of the responsibility so much better. What does this mean for you, builder? It means it's okay to rest. It means it's okay if you get it wrong. It means it's okay to move without the full picture. It means it's okay to tag a friend. The key is to ensure that we build with the architect, the master builder, because there will be a testing of what has been built.

I Corinthians 3:10–15 (AMP), [10] According to the [remarkable] grace of God which was given to me [to prepare me for my task], like a skillful master builder I laid a foundation, and now another is building on it. But each one must be careful how he builds on it, [11] for no one can lay a foundation other than the one which is [already] laid, which is Jesus Christ. [12] But if anyone builds on the foundation with gold, silver, precious stones, wood, hay, straw, [13] each one's work will be clearly shown [for what it is]; for the day [of judgment] will disclose it, because it is to be revealed with fire, *and* the fire will test the quality and character *and* worth of each person's work. [14] If any person's work which he has built [on this foundation, that is, any outcome of his effort] remains [and survives this test], he will receive a reward. [15] But if any person's work is burned up [by the test], he will suffer the loss [of his reward]; yet he himself will be saved, but only as [one who has barely escaped] through fire.

Build the Team, Achieve the Dream

by Gary Ellick[9]

We've all heard phrases such as:
"Teamwork makes the dream work." "There's no 'I' in team."

As a college athlete, military service member, coach, and business owner, my ability to succeed was/is directly dependent on my team. I adopted the phrase, "build the team, achieve the dream," as a teenager. I recognized that as a team captain, my success was connected to my ability to lead and develop my teammates. No matter the amount of talent I possessed, I needed my teammates to achieve the goals I had as an athlete. I took the same mentality into the military, and I still use it today as a coach and business owner.

Since you are reading this book, I believe you are a person with a great vision. You've been burdened by this idea that keeps you up at night. You think about it when you're driving to work, when you're in the gym, and when you're at the dinner table. You know exactly what it looks like and you know it's going to be successful. You also know there are many moving parts needed to bring this vision to life. You often ask, *how am I going to do all of this?* You recognize there are areas you aren't skilled in, but that are vital to your vision's success. Let's get straight to it. You need a team! With every story of greatness, you will find a great team behind the scenes.

Creating a team may seem like a daunting task. Some think of the money they will have to spend to pay someone for service. Let's simplify this. Start with your circle. If you're just starting out building your vision, one of the most important things is having people around you who are trustworthy and dependable. Yes, you will need people with technical skill sets who can deliver specific services. You also need people that you are able to share your heart with. They are just as important as the people who provide technical skills. These people allow you to do "brain-dumps" at 2 a.m. and they help you sift through all of those ideas. These people help you carry the load of this vision.

To build an effective team, you must select the right people. This may sound like a simple task, but many overlook what it means to have the right people. Someone may be highly skilled but lack self-discipline and a team player attitude. While they may provide a great service, they bring the morale of your team down, which brings the overall productivity down with your team. A bad apple that goes unchecked could lead to the failure of this team. So, it's important not to just look for the technical skills, but we also want people that possess the soft skills that mesh with the team. This will be dependent on you as a leader. It will hinge on your ability to communicate the vision and mission of your business/organization to people.

There have been times when I acquired new partnerships from being able to clearly communicate what my business/organization is, what we do, and where we want to go. I was authentic in my delivery. I was clear about what I wanted to do. They could hear the passion and why I wanted to do what I was doing. There must be clarity in the communication of the vision. When selecting your team, you must ensure that what you are doing is meaningful to them. If the mission is meaningful to them, and the vision is clear to them, then this increases the likelihood of their commitment to the business/organization.

To select the right team, you must assess the kind of leader you are as well. This will have a great impact on the personality types of the team members. For example, if you are a non-confrontational person or you just don't do well in conflict, you may want one or two team members that excel in conflict resolution. One thing that you cannot avoid within the team is conflict. Conflict is good. It shows that your team has not fallen victim to groupthink. Conflict can also be damaging to a team when it is not managed well. If the mismanagement of conflict becomes a habitual behavior of the team, then failure is unavoidable in the future.

The assessment of yourself as a leader in your business, as a whole, should be something that happens periodically. This will give you the best picture of what kind of team you need for the season you are currently in or are about to enter into. As your business/organization grows, there will be less that you can manage with your own two hands. If this lesson can be learned early, you can avoid major headaches down the road. Selecting the right team is important, and once you have that team, you must possess the character and skill set to develop and retain this team. This is where many leaders fail. One of the most impactful things you can do is **empower your team**. This requires a leader to be able to relinquish control and delegate tasks and activities to team members. One of the easiest ways to suck the life out of an energetic and productive team is to be a micromanaging, domineering leader. Most times, this comes from a leader's lack of trust of the team, as well as the insecurity of a leader.

When consulting with organizations, I've found leaders will recognize a team member can complete a task, but will refuse to delegate authority to the team member to do so. This refusal stemmed from a fear of the team member performing better than they would. There was also fear of that team member gaining more influence than that of the leader. Many times, I observed this behavior. It wasn't due to the poor performance of the team that created the trust issues. It was rooted in the character of the leader. I have witnessed this in the sports world, in the military, and in business.

The key lesson I learned was to constantly develop my character. This required me to do a deep dive in learning about myself. I learned to do this early in my life as a teenager because I desired to be the best team captain and I wanted to win. I knew winning was impossible on my own. I felt being the best leader for my guys could result in them being the best teammates for me. I took the same approach in the military.

Every quarter I would ask my sailors their likes, dislikes, what I did well, and where I could improve. I asked them to be brutally honest, and they were. I use this with family as well. The only way I can lead my team better as a husband and father is to hear the truth about my performance from my wife and kids.

Overall, you can select the right team, but you must have the right character to develop and retain this team. You are building a God-given vision, and the truth is it's too big for you to do with only your two hands. There are already pre-ordained people set on the path to connect with you. You must do the work to first seek God and His wisdom in choosing the team members to help build in this season. The enemy desires to thwart God's plan through the use of counterfeits infiltrating your team. They will sound good. They will dress well and they will be skilled, but they will not be for YOUR team. You will be able to discern this. Begin to assess your character. Meditate and pray this scripture:

> *Psalm 139:23-24*
> *[23] Search me, O God, and know my heart; test me and know my anxious thoughts. [24] Point out anything in me that offends you, and lead me along the path of everlasting life.*

Continually fine tune your character. What you are building is needed and world changing! Let's get to work!

Be UNIQUELY You!

by Dr. Charlene Winley[10]

Words of Wisdom for Kingdompreneurs

If I can give one word of wisdom, it is to be UNIQUELY you!

Know that God created you:

- On purpose

- With a purpose

- For a purpose

You are not a mistake, an afterthought, or here by happenstance. You are divinely called for such a time as this. Let everything you do pour from this vein.

Jeremiah 1:4–10 NLT states:

[4] The LORD gave me this message: [5] "I knew you before I formed you in your mother's womb. Before you were born I set you apart and appointed you as my prophet to the nations." [6] "O Sovereign LORD," I said, "I can't speak for you! I'm too young!" [7] The LORD replied, "Don't say, 'I'm too young,' for you must go wherever I send you and

say whatever I tell you. [8] And don't be afraid of the people, for I will be with you and will protect you. I, the LORD, have spoken!" [9] Then the LORD reached out and touched my mouth and said, "Look, I have put my words in your mouth! [10] Today, I appoint you to stand up against nations and kingdoms. Some you must uproot and tear down, destroy and overthrow. Others you must build up and plant."

Your voice is unique for this time and season. Do not try to mimic a sound or method by others. It is okay to admire someone but never mimic or employ their techniques. If you are going to move and operate as a kingdom specialist, then you need to allow Holy Spirit to develop your unique voice and sound.

Growing up as a bishop's daughter, I did not want to be the example. I didn't want to be the standard for all the girls in the church. I constantly heard, "What will the other girls think if you did this, or you did that?" I wanted to dance. I wanted to be me. I wanted to live my life. Growing up Pentecostal, dancing was forbidden. I couldn't even take dance classes. I felt restricted. Like I didn't have a life. Almost as if I didn't own myself or who I was. The same will happen to you if you do not set your standard and allow others to dictate who you are and what you should do or be. It is time to bring yourself into alignment with your vision and purpose.

You must have a standard from which you will live your life. If you do not, you will be tossed to and fro being a people pleaser and crowd chaser, and you will never release the sound of your voice on the earth.

You will exchange your genius for likes, shares, and follows.

God is not interested in copycats, which is why He delights in variety and in your uniqueness. It is important for you to know that you are called to the Kingdom of God for such a time as this. The people you are called to are looking for you. They are waiting for your sound to awaken them out of their slumber. As a kingdompreneur, you will realize that it's important for you to be authentic. If you are having trouble walking in your authenticity, then spend a couple of days talking to your Heavenly Father. Ask Him what His plan and purpose is for your life. Ask Him to recalibrate you back to His original design, so that you are not walking in the shadow of your former self.

While this may have been your "Modus Operandi," God has been calling things into order and no longer wants you to strategize according to your usual plan. He is saying what worked for you in the last season, will not work for you in this season. I kept hearing Him say, "Trust in Me with ALL of your heart...LEAN NOT TO YOUR UNDERSTANDING. Acknowledge Me in all of your ways...and I WILL DIRECT YOUR PATHS." I ate Proverbs 3:5-6 and Psalms 91:1; Dwell in the secret place, abide under the shadow, like a hungered soul.

Rest - actively allowing the Holy Spirit to lead, guide, and direct your paths.

Restoration - the act of restoring, healing, rebuilding, reclamation, recovery, reestablishment, reformation, rehabilitation, rejuvenation, remaking, remodeling, renewal, renovation, return, and revival.

He is divinely aligning and bringing things back into order. This means things may have to go out of order or chaotic for a season. What happens when you spring clean? The process of spring cleaning causes your house to become in complete disarray—out of order to bring back into order. During this process, it certainly does not look like what you had in mind. In fact, it is worse than before you began. A thorough examination tells you...man, I have a lot of work to do. You know that when you are finished scrubbing the walls, floors, and baseboards, washing windows, cleaning out the closets, giving things away, and throwing out the trash, you will almost have a brand-new home. Things you have accumulated over the past few years have lost their meaning and value and you can begin to discard them. They are no longer functional in your life in this season.

So it is in the spiritual. The Holy Spirit is saying, I have examined some places and there are necessary changes—things, habits, formulas, strategies, and traditions—which need to be discarded so I can execute My purpose and plan in this season. I will cause the chaos to come into order. It is a new season. Many things you are carrying over from the last season are not necessary and are perhaps a hindrance. What need do you have for a heavy winter coat in the spring or summer weather? People will think you are having an emotional moment, wearing a coat in ninety-degree weather. It matters not where you purchased the coat or how much you paid for it, the fact remains that it is not functional now. Trying to wear it in this season will cause you to be very uncomfortable because you are trying to make something from a past season work in the new season.

God is calling you into DIVINE alignment. He wants you to look at the cracks in your foundation and reinforce them. No need to build on a foundation that cannot support where God wants to take you.

Do not worry about the greater things. Focus on going deeper and HE will cause you to go higher.

Find that secret place...abide in HIS shadow. Rest in HIM. TRUST HIM.

Psalm 40:1(AMP), I WAITED patiently and expectantly for the Lord; And He inclined to me and heard my cry (Biblegateway.com).

Be UNIQUELY YOU and He'll take care of everything else.

Keep in Touch:
www.facebook.com/charlenedwinley
www.facebook.com/drcharlenedwinley
www.twitter.com/charlenedwinley
www.instagram.com/charlenedwinley
www.charlenedwinley.com

F.A.T | Faithful-Available-Teachable

by Robert Bennet Jr.[11]

If ye be willing and obedient, ye shall eat the good of the land: But if you refuse and rebel, you shall be devoured by the sword"; For the mouth of the LORD has spoken.

Today, everyone is trying to be fit rather than healthy. With fad diets and the repudiation of the gym, some prefer the least resistance. However, just like anything else, healthy living requires discipline. It requires commitment, patience, and endurance to achieve the goal of personal satisfaction. True to form, only you will know if you have reached your goal or failed at trying. As a leader, the same can be said about your leadership and the direction of your company, organization, or family. Leaders have the daunting task of galvanizing the people they serve to ensure that goals and objectives are met. More importantly, the systems put in place work and are effective. My tenure as a servant leader has afforded me opportunities to work with a myriad of individuals and organizations to achieve maximum efficacy and resolve. No, I'm not a health guru or a fitness nut, but for the sake of enlightenment, I want you to consider being "Faithful, Available, Teachable," FAT. For some, that's an unscrupulous term. It's derogatory and off-putting, however, it speaks to the essence of what we need to be successful. Growing up in church was the ultimate training and development I needed to sharpen my leadership and people skills.

Life lessons and experiences have yielded measurable results, which set the foundation for positive change. Proverbs 28:20 says, "A faithful man will abound with blessings." Faithfulness is a learned skill. One would think it is a personality trait, but in fact, it is a skill that can be harnessed. Faithfulness is the concept of unfailing loyalty to someone or something that bears consistency regardless of extenuating circumstances. Faithfulness is measured by motive, engineered by "why," why you do the things you do. Being faithful illustrates your ability to trust processes. Now, because of faithfulness, you qualify for blessings. All promises outlined in the Bible are conditioned based on an exchange. It's like one plus one, well, we know that equals two, so being faithful equals blessings. When leaders are loyal to their craft, team, or organization, they unlock blessings from the top down. Abound is defined as, "To occur or exist in great quantities or numbers; to be rich or well supplied; to be filled." When we are faithful, we will be rich, well supplied, and filled with God's blessings in more ways than we can imagine. Now, being faithful is only a third of the equation. Arguably, availability is paramount. You can be faithful and teachable but if you are absent, it leaves a void.

> *1 Samuel 3:4*
> *"The Lord called Samuel: and he answered, 'Here am I.'"*

Availability is not just about showing up. Yes, showing up is half the battle when it comes to leadership, organizing, and a healthy work-life balance. People who are not available to see the vision through are a metaphoric cancer. Cancer eats away at the good cells and tissues, which creates a defect, and its growth has an adverse effect on the overall schema. Bad habits tend to spread faster than good ones. The moment you lack decorum, respect is eroded, and the impropriety rears its ugly head.

It is the responsibility of the leader to always be the first partaker in being available. Creating a culture of "do as I say, and not as I do" is a recipe for deficiency. If the organization, or church, or even your family, can't depend on you as the leader, it is certain that the mission, objective, or nucleus will fail. So often we hear the phrase "leaders lead by example," but I would like to challenge that notion and say leaders are the example. As a leader you must "BE" what you want to manifest. In other words, you must identify with what you want to see manifested. Fully engage, submerge, and most importantly, be true to yourself, with room for grace.

If you want your leaders on time for meetings, you must be on time. If you want your leaders to be kind to staff, members, and clients, you must show yourself to be kind. Lastly, if you want your leaders to work hard, you must be the leader that they see working hard. Your availability to your leaders solidifies your validity as luminary. To fully achieve and become the best leader, you must consider your self-awareness. Being available and self-aware requires you to be spiritually, mentally, physically, socially, and emotionally stable. Ask yourself the hard questions, "Am I doing this right? How can I improve myself? Who can I pour into now? What's the next book I can read to prepare my mind for the next opportunity?" Being self-aware shows who you are and who you desire to become.

Faithfulness opens doors, availability makes room for more, but being teachable requires humility. To be teachable, one must exhibit humility and vulnerability. Humility to say, "I don't know everything," and the vulnerability to say, "I need help." They truly go hand in hand. Being teachable allows you to be a conduit of change. No matter the concept or challenge, or how much subject matter you know, you must be willing to listen to another perspective and be respectful. At times, we can discredit message(s) because we don't like the messenger. The true essence of a teachable person is one who uses critical thinking. Critical thinking requires you to synthesize, analyze, apply previous knowledge, and balance your thought process. Leaders who are teachable aren't just learning but they are becoming subject matter experts in people, concepts, and ideas. I always want to be in a room full of people who know more than me. Again, being teachable requires humility and vulnerability. Not knowing it all allows for growth and maturity. Ingest and implement all that you can for maximum growth. Don't allow what you don't know to intimidate you. Your job is to grow and share best practices. Your ability to be a change agent allows for others to follow your example to not be intimidated. Lastly, keep an open mind. There's a saying "closed mouths don't get fed." I'd like to add, a closed mind doesn't get fed either.

I started this chapter by saying "if you are willing and obedient you will eat the good of the land." Being FAT requires obedience and a willingness to try. Are you willing to indulge yourself in the delicacies of being teachable, making yourself available, and anchoring your efforts with faithfulness? The requirements of success lie in your willingness to allow yourself to be FAT (Faithful, Available & Teachable). Rid yourself of the opinions of others, lay aside the tendencies of looking well instead of being well. This is your moment to allow God to enlarge your territory through focus sprinkled with flavor. Let's eat!

A Builder's Time & Grace

by Erica Ojada[12]

Ecclesiastes 3:1 (AMP)
"There is a season (a time appointed) for everything and a time for every delight and event or purpose under heaven."

God has set a release date for what He burdens you to build. I believe sometimes as builders we get so caught up in the pressure of producing that the how becomes too weighty and we cannot hear God's instructions. This is the perfect time for us to stop everything and seek God. Remove the demand from yourself and place the demand on God. I always start off by asking God, what's Your will? How do you want this done? And then I increase my faith by knowing if He has said it, then so shall it be. This removes the external pressures and allows you to refocus. God wants to build with you. He has entrusted you with the burden to build and He will give you the grace to build it. We must follow His leading because the very thing He purposed in our hearts to build is on a time release. It serves a particular purpose for a time to fulfill God's will.

I had a burden to teach people to pray and intercede more. I saw the lack of prayer in the ministry and it drove me wild. I understood the purpose and effectiveness of prayer, and it truly grieved me to see my brothers or sisters live below God's standard of life because they did not know how to petition heaven for themselves. At the time, the prayer department was a small group of people and was a department most people didn't sign up for. I was only a member of the prayer department, not a leader. God gave me a burden, but I was not yet in a position to execute the very thing that weighed heavy in my heart. What do you do when you have a burden to build a thing but don't have access or authority yet to execute and build it in your position? I couldn't go to the leader of the group and demand I teach or overthrow the leader and teach on the side. I had to wait on God's timing. I took what was burning inside of me to do and submitted my burden back to God. I laid it back on the altar and prayed for God to give me understanding, wisdom, and instructions on how to move. Although there was an immediate need for the burden within me, it wasn't yet time for me to launch.

> **Nehemiah 1:4 (NKJV)**
> *"So it was, when I heard these words, that I sat down and wept, and mourned for many days; I was fasting and praying before the God of heaven."*

Nehemiah became very concerned with the state of Jerusalem. The wall and gates were ruined, and he was burdened to rebuild them. Although Nehemiah had a burden and there was an immediate need, he sought God first because he was a captive of the king and needed permission. While Nehemiah was praying and fasting, God was working on the king's heart to release Nehemiah to go rebuild. Whenever God gives you a burden and you are not able to act on that burden, you need God's grace. To have God's grace, you need to move in God's time. To move in God's time, you need to seek God's will. If God hasn't graced you yet for the build, you will be working in your own might and power instead of God's spirit. If He has burdened you, He will provide all that you need to succeed.

While I was waiting for God to release me to lead and teach, I started to prepare myself. I started to read books on prayer and study because I knew once God released me to build, I wouldn't have the time to read and study as much. Whenever we are waiting on God for a release, that is the best time for us to prepare. We must work on our character to lead, strengthen our inner man, increase our faith, and pray. Yes, pray even more. Let that burden burn on the altar before God so the intention of building stays pure, and is for the Glory of God and the building of the Kingdom.

Once Nehemiah received the release from the king, he started to prepare. He asked for letters. One letter permitted Nehemiah to travel and build the wall and the other letter gave him access to materials needed to build. We should prepare to be physically, spiritually, and mentally strong for the process ahead. I started to ask God to give me the mind of a great leader, to give me a new perspective on people, and to give me compassion for the people I am called to lead. Months down the line, I was promoted to co-leader of the prayer department. Often times, God is waiting on our preparation before He promotes us. The ability to prepare and ready ourselves lets God know we are ready for our next.

Once I became a co-lead of the prayer department, I performed an assessment. I met with the leader and asked, "What are your pain points with the team? What do you need help with? Are you open to new ideas for the team?" Yes, you have a burden, and yes, it may seem like it's the perfect time to set up shop, but it is imperative to perform an assessment. It was not my time, because my role was to support, not to take over. I needed to understand how we started, where we were currently, and what our future was. The truth of the matter is, God gave the leader a burden too, and my first job was to assist the leader with fulfilling God's mandate.

In Nehemiah Chapter 2, Nehemiah assessed the damage to the wall and gates, gathered the people, and encouraged them to rebuild the walls, so they all set their minds to build the wall and gates. Being of one mind is so important when building. My take on the matter is, it doesn't matter who is leading, just as long as we are building the Kingdom. It's important to know when you should be serving a vision or leading a vision. God tested my heart to see if I would submit. Even though I had this burning burden within me, I submitted myself until God's appointed time.

By the next year, I was appointed leader of the prayer department. It was now the appointed time for me to act on the burden that God placed on my heart. It was time for me to take the department to the next level. I prayed even more because now, I needed the grace to lead, teach, and fulfill God's mandate. The builder's grace is empowerment, endurance, resilience, and most importantly, complete trust in God. Now that I was in position, I understood there was going to be some opposition. But because I waited on God, I knew His grace was sufficient enough to keep me while I was building. Although I was in my appointed time to build, that did not mean I was free from attacks and opposition. But because I prepared and waited, I knew I was also graced to fight.

In Nehemiah Chapter 4, while building the wall, Nehemiah and the builders had some opposition and attacks. But because God graced them to complete the work, they only needed to pray, watch, and prepare to fight. On the one hand, they built, and on the other hand, they readied their weapons. God's burden needs God's timing, which will release the builder's grace to build and will ensure God's will fulfilled on earth through you.

NEXT

by Andre Mason[13]

If you're reading this, then somewhere in the recesses of your heart, you've unearthed a yearning for more. A desire for "next." Although what "next" looks like may be extremely foggy at this time, you have a strong pull to uncover it. I've been there. It started with the small, nagging unction that "more" existed. Soon, I was wrestling with a vision that I knew wasn't quite my own. A divine download began consistently loosing the hardwired programming that I adapted from my environment, my upbringing, my and education. I stopped understanding my salary, in comparison to how much I produced for the company I worked for. It eventually evolved into sleepless nights. I spent those calculating how to close the gap between where I was and this seemingly elusive, although extremely compelling, future. My path was leading me to a future that revealed me living a life as a full-time entrepreneur. Yours may be different. You may be reading this with no desire to plunge headfirst into the wacky world of full-time entrepreneurship. You may feel an unction toward a nobler task, like starting a nonprofit to help feed the homeless, or a call as a pastor or minister in the Lord's church. No matter the call, the thing I want to share with you will serve as a gem of paramount importance as you pursue what's next.

Years ago, when I felt the call to leave the employee workforce, the perspective on where I was going and how I would get there was very linear. My mental blueprint looked like this: Step 1. Leave the job. Step 2. Prospect new clients for my already established business. Step 3. Count the money/live the dream! I assumed that the transition to next would make use of all the tools that I had sharpened during my tenure in sales. At the time, I had already been operating as a part-time entrepreneur, so I welcomed the chance to give the full-time thing a try. Then, the Lord spoke to me. He gave me some additional insight into my "next." He told me that he wanted me to document the journey, so that those like you, who would soon emerge as entrepreneurs or leaders, would also have some intel on what to expect as you transition. He even gave me a name for it. At the time, what I thought would be an album turned out to be my first book, Freedom Papers. It's set to release in the months before this anthology. That wasn't just a shameless plug, although, I'm grateful for whatever support I may receive. I wanted to share that tidbit so as to pinpoint the moment when my linear plan would become very crooked. To be quite frank, I had anticipated that the transition would challenge my skills more than it would my character. Friend, I was wrong.

In my opinion, the biggest threat to whether or not you will successfully transition into your "next," is not how well you execute and deploy your developed skills. The biggest threat to whether or not you see your "next" is how you steward the undeveloped parts of your character. Friend, the more I talk to entrepreneurs and leaders, emerging, established, or otherwise, the more I discover the prominence of this one common thread. Adversity, EXTREME, tailor-fit adversity. The children of Israel had it in the wilderness. They were afraid of war (Exodus 13:17). They were free. They could've walked into their next within a few days, but one of the reasons that they did not is because they had undeveloped character. Fear and disobedience would become Israel's sparring partners while in the wilderness. God would use each encounter to prep them for next. God knows that entering you into your next prematurely would be to your detriment, so He ensures that you are developed. I'm willing to bet that if you did the research, every successful person you've grown to admire has had to endure their own tailor-fit wilderness. I'd also venture to bet that not one of them regrets it. In my personal wilderness, I've dealt with mental anguish, a repossessed vehicle, a near foreclosure, displacement from fire, a completely demolished credit score, and a whole host of other issues. One thing that I can say is that I wouldn't trade the fruit of those experiences for anything. If I'm honest, I didn't understand why I was being met with so much opposition, both internal and external, as I followed what I truly felt was the Lord's will for me. Soon though, as I continued my journey, I began to welcome every challenge. You see, my personal wilderness was about faith and trust. When I embarked on the journey to full-time entrepreneurship, I thought I had faith in God, and I did, but those levels of faith were commensurate with where I had been, not where I was going. I didn't have faith to trust God in my finances beyond what my eyes could see, so He had to develop that. I didn't have faith to truly trust that despite where I was emotionally, and even physically, that God was still there, so He allowed resistance to develop what I lacked. These things had to be developed. God's weapon of choice to produce maturity is suffering.

> *James 1:2–4 reads like this: ²Consider it pure joy, my brothers and sisters,[a] whenever you face trials of many kinds, ³ because you know that the testing of your faith produces perseverance. ⁴ Let perseverance finish its work so that you may be mature and complete, not lacking anything.*

Most people shun suffering and that is precisely why they remain stagnant and unable to fully pursue their next. It's because when introduced to the sparring partner of suffering and adversity, they view it as a sign that they've heard wrong, chosen wrong, or planned wrong. The truth is, when God introduces adversity, He's introducing opportunity. Opportunity to become mature in an area that needs development. This has been the separating line for those who attain success and those who live with the regret of not pressing past discomfort. When listening to interviews with the most successful builders, they will clue the keen listener into some of the hardships that they had to overcome to become who they are. After a while, you can unlock a common theme. These wise souls have unlocked the wisdom in understanding that failure, trial, and adversity are the admission price for success. Most emerging leaders and emerging entrepreneurs aren't introduced to this concept until they are well on the road to next. But the benefit of having this information upfront is that it will help accelerate you to "next" by eliminating the time you spend trying to figure out "why" a chain of adverse events has occurred. I couldn't blame you for not being able to see how Paul would admonish the reader to "count it pure joy" when you face trials. Embracing pain is an extremely counterintuitive concept. Truth is, though, some portions of our character have been restricted from the pruning and the deep work of the spirit of God. Understanding upfront that Godly suffering produces perseverance and maturity and approaching it with a joyful mindset will produce a resilience that you didn't know you needed. Israel had enough faith to pray but not enough to fight, and that proved to be a problem because they, like most of us, were going into an occupied space. Spaces filled with powers, board members, strongholds, and all types of opposition that won't be too fond of someone like you entering with a new mandate, a new direction, a new vision for the organization, etc. When you meet resistance, it's paramount that you possess the resilience of a fortified, fire-tested character.

ARCHITECTS

Meet the Architects

Meet the Architects

1   Scan to Connect with Torace Solomon:

2   Scan to Connect with Pastor Jeff Wittaker:

3   Scan to Connect with Elouise Townsend:

4   Scan to Connect with Luis Trochez:

5 Scan to Connect with Lakia Perez:

6 Scan to Connect with Justin Goodman:

7 Scan to Connect with Ciara Mason:

8 Scan to Connect with Dr. Chavon Anette:

9   Scan to Connect with Gary Ellick:

10 Scan to Connect with Dr. Charlene Winley:

11 Scan to Connect with Robert Bennet Jr.:

12 Scan to Connect with Erica Ojada:

13   Scan to Connect with Andre Mason:

14   Scan to Connect with Visionary Kiyanni Bryan:

Made in the USA
Columbia, SC
24 February 2025